MW01483999

25 DEVOTIONAL READINGS

WEARY WORLD REJOICE!

FOR ADVENT & CHRISTMAS

MOUNTAIN LIFE PUBLISHING

25 DEVOTIONAL READINGS

WEARY WORLD REJOICE!

FOR ADVENT & CHRISTMAS

NATE MORRIS

25 DEVOTIONAL READINGS

WEARY WORLD REJOICE!

FOR ADVENT & CHRISTMAS

Copyright ©2020 by Nathanael E. Morris (Nate Morris)
https://pastorn8.com
Instagram: @natemorris1
Facebook: nate.morris.9047

Published by Mountain Life Publishing
https://mountainlife.church
225 Main St. #G-003
Edwards, CO 81632

ISBN: 9781737921707
First Printing, 2021

TABLE OF CONTENTS

ACKNOWLEDGEMENTS

I am so grateful to my Lord for the privilege of being His child and for His hand in this process. I would not have even begun this project without Him prodding me along.

I am thankful for my voluntary editor, Norrie Bush. Without Norrie, this book would be much more difficult to read and communicate my heart with much less clarity.

I am thankful for my church, Mountain Life Calvary Chapel, and for our wonderful staff, who have supported the publication of this book and given my life inspiration for its contents.

Lastly, I am grateful beyond words for my wife, Jen, and my three kids, Caleb, Zoe, and Josiah, who fill my world with wonder, joy, and life.

PROLOGUE

Life is a constant rollercoaster of ups and downs. This has been especially true in recent years. The arrival of social media, the reality of terrorism and war, a season of increasingly divisive politics, and the ongoing pandemic have left us with a weary world.

So what does an Advent devotional have to do with all that? Well, while I love Christmastime, I've never really latched on to the celebration of the Advent tradition (the period of waiting and expectation that leads to Christmas.) However, the past few years have changed that for me. I now understand Advent as I never have before, and I've begun to embrace the patient expectation and ache of longing for the fulfillment of God's promise in my life and our world.

This daily devotional journey will walk us through the advent season as we embrace the ache we have to be made whole and realize Jesus as the present and future fulfillment of this hope. I pray it blesses you, as it has blessed me to write it.

- Pastor Nate Morris

DAY 1

Embracing the ache of Advent

Advent is a season set aside to symbolize the time of waiting, watching, and hoping for the coming of the Messiah. It is a symbol of the Jewish people longing for the birth of their Messiah. Advent also represents the enduring anticipation of Christians for the second coming of Jesus.

Advent has never really captured my heart before. I've always understood what it meant, but it never resonated with me - until 2020. When the COVID-19 pandemic hit, things changed. The fallout from the pandemic resulted in political unrest, increased racial tension and deep division not only in the world, but even in the church. 2020, and the time since, has been a constant aching and longing for things to get better. For the first time, I can identify with what the Jewish People felt as they awaited their Messiah, the one who would set all wrongs right.

As a Christian, I know that Jesus fulfills that aching, longing, and waiting for me. This is spiritually true today, and will be physically true when He makes all things new in His Kingdom (*Revelation 21)*! This is why I've never really grasped the heart of Advent, because I already know Jesus, and He's already transformed my life. So, what's with all the aching and waiting stuff?

But after 2020, things were different. I have been reminded in a new way of the truth found in *Romans 8:22*, which says that the whole creation aches and groans to see the redemption that is coming. This is what I'm feeling now. Like never before, I want to see Jesus come and set things right, right now.

For today, Day 1 of Advent, embrace the ache. Take a moment and allow yourself to see that without Jesus this world has no hope. This may sound fatalistic and bleak to you, but it's truly the most hopeful realization we can reach. How so? Who else but Jesus is worth putting our hope in? Presidents, governors, politicians, celebrities, and even family and friends will let us down - and probably already have, many times. Jesus is the only one who will never let us down! If I have to entrust the future to someone, let it be to Him.

So embrace the ache for more. Embrace the brokenness in longing for the future hope that will be revealed to us, and in us, at the second coming of Jesus. Embrace what Paul wrote in *Romans 8:23*.

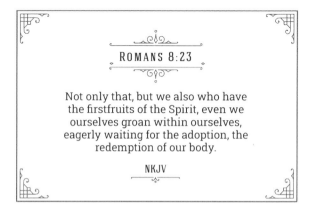

ROMANS 8:23

Not only that, but we also who have the firstfruits of the Spirit, even we ourselves groan within ourselves, eagerly waiting for the adoption, the redemption of our body.

NKJV

DAY 2

ACHING FOR OUR TRUE COUNTRY

Yesterday we talked about embracing the ache of Advent, longing for the coming of our King, and for Him to make all things new again. Today we continue in exploring that theme. As we do, I'd like to take a moment and highlight why it is we groan for a better world (as we read in *Romans 8:22-23*), and why we long for something more.

Jesus said that we are "not of this world", and as much as I value being a United States citizen, I know that my citizenship here is truly secondary. I belong to another country; a heavenly country with a heavenly King.

As C.S. Lewis explores in his book Mere Christianity, human beings seem to have innate needs and thirsts that cannot be quenched by the things or experiences of this world. The best explanation for these yearnings is that we were made for a different world. The fact that experiences in this life do not fully satisfy my desire should not be discouraging, but rather remind me that my true country is waiting for me, I have only to press through my disappointment to get there.

This longing for our true country is the central theme of the advent season. Our patient waiting and longing for the joy of Christmas parallels our longing and waiting for our true home.

What joys await all who look forward to new bodies, and a new heaven and earth, exactly as our Lord has promised! This hope gives us the strength to press on, even as we face the brokenness and hopelessness in the world around us.

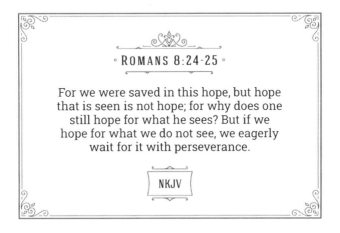

· ROMANS 8:24-25 ·

For we were saved in this hope, but hope that is seen is not hope; for why does one still hope for what he sees? But if we hope for what we do not see, we eagerly wait for it with perseverance.

NKJV

As you face disappointments in life, allow them to remind you that you don't belong here. You belong to another country, a heavenly country. And when you go home, every disappointment you face today will be like a bad dream, long-forgotten in the beauty of the morning sun.

DAY 3

ACHING FOR RESTORATION

As we explored yesterday, part of the reason we long for things to be different is because we don't belong here! We are not of this world, and we are waiting to go home to our True Country. But in another sense, it is not just another world we long for, as it's also the restoration of this one. You see, this world is not as it was meant to be, which Paul explains beautifully in *Romans 8:19-21.*

Romans 8:19-21 (NKJV)
For the earnest expectation of the creation eagerly waits for the revealing of the sons of God. For the creation was subjected to futility, not willingly, but because of Him who subjected it in hope; because the creation itself also will be delivered from the bondage of corruption into the glorious liberty of the children of God.

Notice that it is not just you and I waiting for God's redemption, creation itself is also eagerly awaiting the same thing. The ache that we all feel for a better world, and for all wrongs to be made right, is completely natural. The reason things don't feel right in this world is because they are not right. So it's natural for us to feel that longing; that aching for restoration. It's natural because the current state of our world is not natural; it's not how God created it...we've messed it all up. Mankind's sin and selfishness has ruined everything. I am a big Charlie Brown Christmas fan. It's one of my favorite Christmas traditions, and has been since I was a kid. Every year my family and I gather around the TV and enjoy the nostalgia and humor, with the clear presentation of the gospel that it offers. If you've never seen it, I highly recommend watching it this year, and looking for the themes of Advent we've been discussing.

There is a part in the special where Charlie Brown is attempting to celebrate the real meaning of Christmas, and he buys this bare, dinky little Christmas tree. And, as he's decorating it, it falls over, and he exclaims "Everything I touch gets ruined!"

That may or may not have been true for Charlie Brown, but in a real sense it is true for humanity. Everything we touch gets ruined. Yes, we do see glimmers of hope in acts of kindness, or in selfless sacrifices every once in a while. However, it only takes a day or two to be reminded of the depths of human depravity in ways that make our hearts hurt. Our world is broken, and it's only getting worse. This is why we long for something more; this is why we need a savior, a redeemer.

Thankfully, for those of us who are followers of Christ, we know the end of the story. We know our redeemer lives, and that He was not only born into this world, but is also coming back to rebuild, redeem, and restore it. He will bring our True Country to this fallen world, and set things right for eternity!

Hold fast to that hope of God's restoration today. Let the longing you have for more stir your heart to praise Him Who is coming indeed.

DAY 4

CREATION LONGS WITH US

Part of the reason we notice such a clear contrast in our hearts between the ideal and the real, what we long to see versus what we do see, is because God has given mankind over to the mess we're in. We read in *Romans 1:24* that He gave mankind up to uncleanness, and we see in *Romans 8:20* that creation was subjected to futility, to the bondage of corruption. What this means is that as sin separated us from God, He not only gave us over to the dominion of sin, but He put creation under that same dominion of sin as well. This is why creation only reveals a glimmer or hint of the goodness of God, even as beautiful as it is. We see the beauty of creation, and at the same time we see the ugliness of disease, death, and brutality.

I really believe God intends, or at the very least uses, this fallen state of creation to arouse in us the desire for the way it was meant to be. When we look at the world around us, we are struck by competing truths. First, we see the glory of God and His eternal power (*Romans 1:20*), and at the same time we see the fallen state of our world. When these two truths take root in our hearts, they reveal that something is wrong; something is broken and needs to be fixed. When we see the ravages of death and disease our hearts ache for the life that God intended. In His infinite wisdom, God has put eternity

in the human heart (*Ecclesiastes 3:11*), so that the contrast-
ing truths of beauty and brokenness stir us to look and long
for something better. Thanks be to God that there is a future
and a hope to look forward to, not only for us humans but for
creation as well. In the same section of Romans 8 that we've
been reading, it says that He has subjected creation in hope,
because it will be delivered into the liberty of the children of
God. Isaiah 11:6-9 describes what this redemption of creation
will look like:

Isaiah 11:6–9 (NKJV)
"The wolf also shall dwell with the lamb, the leopard shall lie down
with the young goat, the calf and the young lion and the fatling
together; and a little child shall lead them. The cow and the bear shall
graze; their young ones shall lie down together; and the lion shall eat
straw like the ox. The nursing child shall play by the cobra's hole, and
the weaned child shall put his hand in the viper's den. They shall not
hurt nor destroy in all My holy mountain, for the earth shall be full of
the knowledge of the Lord as the waters cover the sea."

It's hard to imagine this scene to be real, but this is because
of the jaded hearts we have in this fallen world. Yet it also
strikes a chord within us because something about it rings
true, like a long-forgotten memory or dream, but glimpsed
in the moment. I am thankful that in the end, the forgotten
dream, or distant memory will be the long season of ache and
longing we are currently in. The ideal will become the real,
and darkness will be swallowed up in light. Our hope will be
hope no more, as it will be true life like we've never known!

As we walk through this Advent season, with whatever
distractions and stresses are on your mind, remember that
the brokenness of our world only highlights the goodness of
God, and the hope we have in Him.

Choose to *"rest your hope fully upon the grace that is to be brought to*
you at the revelation of Jesus Christ;" – 1 Peter 1:13 (NKJV)

DAY 5

LONGING FOR FULL REDEMPTION

We've been talking about how the state of the world causes our hearts to ache for the redemption of God, when He will set all things right. I think we can all identify with that in our world today. So much has gone on around us that causes our hearts to break. But it's not just the circumstances and the heartaches we see in the world around us that causes our longing for His promise, it is also what goes on inside of us.

Yes, the world around us is broken and fallen, but if we are honest with ourselves, so are we. If I have put my faith in Jesus, I trust I am saved, cleansed, and forgiven, and I know that I have eternal life. God has made me new, and I am being made more and more into the image of Jesus every day. Yet, I still carry around with me my old self, who is perishing. (2 Corinthians 4:16) This "perishing self" that goes with me is what the Bible calls the flesh. Take a look with me at what Galatians 5:17 says about this old self.

Galatians 5:17 (ESV)
For the desires of the flesh are against the Spirit, and the desires of the Spirit are against the flesh, for these are opposed to each other, to keep you from doing the things you want to do.

My flesh is actively attempting to keep me from doing the

things I want and know that I should do in my Spirit. It is waging war against my soul *(1 Peter 2:11).* This battle is continuing day-in and day-out, 24/7, 365 days per year. The current state of the world has only made this fight worse. There have been more opportunities for temptation, fear, anxiety, and responding "in the flesh", than I can recall in recent memory. Let me be the first to tell you, I have not always responded in the Spirit, and done the right thing. What about you?

This constant tension between the perishing of the old and the renewal of the new person is real for all of us, and it is a reminder that though we have been saved and redeemed, we still await our full redemption. We long to be made free from our old person that we call the flesh.

The beauty of Advent is that it highlights both the current and the future deliverance from our flesh. At Christmas we celebrate the birth of Jesus, and ultimately His death for our sins. His death delivered us from the penalty of our sin, but also gave us the Holy Spirit, who delivers us from the power of sin that was over us. Advent reminds us that though I still carry my flesh with me, he is a defeated foe, and I am no longer his slave.

Romans 6:6 (NKJV)
Knowing this, that our old man was crucified with Him, that the body of sin might be done away with, that we should no longer be slaves of sin.

I still have to battle with him daily, but I am fighting from victory, and not for victory. Even when I mess up, give in, or lose a fight, I am not his slave because I am a son of the Most High God. He loves me, and gave Himself for me, so I don't have to cower in defeat. I can stand in the power of the Holy Spirit and know that I am victorious over sin and death in

Jesus. Even though I carry my old person with me, I don't have to go where he leads, as I am set free by the Spirit of God *(Romans 8:12–13)*.

Advent also points us towards our future deliverance. When Jesus returns for His church, we will be changed, fully re-deemed, and fully restored. In that beautiful moment we will no longer have to do battle with our flesh, and we'll no longer be struggling to do the right thing, because we will be truly free.

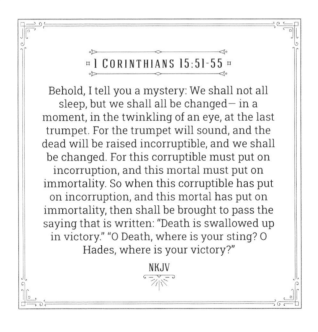

¤ 1 CORINTHIANS 15:51-55 ¤

Behold, I tell you a mystery: We shall not all sleep, but we shall all be changed— in a moment, in the twinkling of an eye, at the last trumpet. For the trumpet will sound, and the dead will be raised incorruptible, and we shall be changed. For this corruptible must put on incorruption, and this mortal must put on immortality. So when this corruptible has put on incorruption, and this mortal has put on immortality, then shall be brought to pass the saying that is written: "Death is swallowed up in victory." "O Death, where is your sting? O Hades, where is your victory?"

NKJV

As you face your own battles today, remember that the gift of Advent is current victory over the power of your flesh, and eventually, complete freedom from it. What a glorious grace we've been given!

DAY 6

LIVING AS A FOREIGNER

As we've established over the past several days, this world is broken and fallen, and in need of redemption and restoration. We long for the day when the wrongs will be made right, the ideal will be the real, and the darkness will be brought into the light. We long for that city, that country, that home that is built by the goodness of God, and not by the brokenness of man. We long for the day our personal redemption will be final and complete as we are received into our True Country, and set free from our old person.

Even though this longing and aching for our True Country can hurt at times, it is a good thing. It keeps us grounded in our destination, the hope of our real home. Which brings me to how we are to live as we wait for our final redemption. How do we live our lives as we see the symbolism in the Advent season; our waiting for the messiah? How do we live our lives in that season of waiting for the Advent of Jesus' return?

We live our lives as foreigners in this world - we live by faith. Abraham is a great example and type of this waiting by faith.

Hebrews 11:8-10 (NKJV)
By faith Abraham obeyed when he was called to go out to the place which he would receive as an inheritance. And he went

out, not knowing where he was going. By faith he dwelt in the land of promise as in a foreign country, dwelling in tents with Isaac and Jacob, the heirs with him of the same promise; 10 for he waited for the city which has foundations, whose builder and maker is God.

Abraham dwelt in the land as a foreigner. He lived as one with confidence in the plan and purpose of God, yet living in a season of waiting for the fulfillment of God's promise. He had his eyes on the city whose builder is God; not himself, not someone else. He lived on this earth as a foreigner, waiting for his True Country. How did he do this? By faith. Abraham's life was a life lived by faith. Not faith that things would get better, but faith in a God who is better. Faith in a God who would keep true to His promise. Faith in a God Who will be Who He says He is, and do what He says He will do.

It is a strange and beautiful truth that when we choose to live by faith as foreigners here on earth, we begin to grasp that we are no longer foreigners in Heaven. As we do, we can experience the full blessing of citizenship in Heaven, even while here on earth.

Whatever you face today, recognize that you are just passing through this place. When that relationship breaks down, when that financial situation causes stress, when that illness or health issue rears its ugly head, when hurt or sorrow or fear or anxiety rises up, take a moment and remember that you are just passing through. Remember that the momentary struggles we face now are but the beginning of amazing stories that we will tell of God's goodness when we get home.

Romans 8:18 (NKJV)
For I consider that the sufferings of this present time are not worthy to be compared with the glory which shall be revealed in us.

DAY 7

HE STEPPED INTO OUR MESS

We've been discussing the aching and longing that we, and all creation have for the redemption God will bring. Things are not OK, and we know it. And so we look forward to the day that our Savior will set all the wrongs right. This is healthy and good, and a significant part of the celebration of Advent - to embrace the longing we have for all things to be made new.

Yet, as we focus on the hope set before us, we can easily miss something that God did, and is doing even now among us. God stepped into our mess. He didn't just sit far off and say "Don't worry, one day I will fix it." He stooped down, condescended to our level, and got His hands dirty and bloody on our behalf. He lived our pain and experienced the ache.

In *Isaiah 7:14,* the prophecy about the messiah says that He will be called Immanuel, which means "God with us". As a 21st century Christian who has had a relationship with God most of my life, I don't naturally grasp the significance of this name. But in Isaiah's day, hundreds of years before Jesus came, this title would have sounded very strange. God with us? How could God be "with us?" God was Holy (meaning other, different, or set apart), God was distant and to be feared. The thought of God being "with us" would have seemed odd, and even offensive.

How could the Almighty, Holy God, possibly stoop so low as to be "with" such low, sinful, wretched creatures as us? Yet, that is exactly what Jesus did. He stepped into our mess. Jesus came and lived in this broken world. He didn't just rescue us out of it, but He experienced the heartache of it. He lived the pain and the sorrow, and He experienced the longing and the aching for redemption. He was "with us," literally. In fact, the Bible tells us that He was tempted in every way that we are, yet was without sin, and so He can sympathize with our weakness, our sorrow, and our heartache (see *Hebrews 4:15*).

This tells me something important. God doesn't just expect us to "grin and bear it" as we go through difficulties in life. He goes through them with us. He was not only "with us" when He came to earth, He is with us even now. He is with you, even as you've messed up and can't see a way out. He is with you as you deal with the consequences of someone else's sin in your life. He is with you as you struggle with loneliness or emptiness. He is with you when you've lost your job, or cannot make your rent payment. He is with you in your struggle with failing health. He is with you as you grieve the loss of your loved one. He is with you, even when no one else is, or will be.

You see, Jesus is not only our future hope, and Advent isn't only about the fact that one day everything will be made right. No, Advent celebrates the fact that He is with us even as we wait and long and ache for more. He is with us in our sorrows and our pain. He is with us when we fall on our face. He is with us as we face a hostile world. He is WITH US.

God is with you today. Whatever your day holds, He is with you. Because of Christmas and because of the cross, He is always with you, even on your worst day. And one day, you will be with Him. What a blessed day that will be!

Hebrews 13:5b (NKJV)
For He Himself has said "I will never leave you nor forsake you."

DAY 8

NOT JUST A FUTURE HOPE A PRESENT ONE

As we patiently await Christmas, celebrating the birth of our King, we are living out an allusion to our patient expectation of Christ's return. This Advent season illustrates our lives lived here on earth: Looking forward to the consummation of God's promise, and our hope fulfilled.

That said, Advent does not remind us only of the future fulfillment of God's promise. It also reminds us of the present reality that God's promises to us are "Yes and amen" for today, as well as tomorrow *(2 Corinthians 1:20)*. As we begin our second week of this Advent journey together, let's remember that we don't only look with expectancy toward the future, but we can experience the goodness of God's promises here and now.

The birth, death, and resurrection of Jesus has secured for us God's exceedingly great and precious promises. Yes, this means promises for eternity, but also promises for today. Take a look at what Peter had to say about these promises.

2 Peter 1:4 (NKJV)
By which have been given to us exceedingly great and precious promises, that through these you may be partakers of the divine nature, having escaped the corruption that is in the world through lust.

Divine nature. We can experience God's power, presence, and blessing today. I think sometimes we forget that we have the Spirit of God living inside us. The Divine nature is literally living inside of you. This is an amazing miracle that I don't fully understand, yet it is a reality that I can experience today and every day. I can partake in His nature today. I can experience hope in Him today. I can experience peace that surpasses understanding today. I can experience freedom from fear and anxiety today. All of these things are available to me today. I just have to choose to partake of His nature to experience them. To partake means to join in. When you partake of a meal, you are digging in and eating. The idea here is that we have the promise of God's nature available to us, and living in us... we just need to partake of Him, to intentionally enjoy our relationship with Him.

As you go through your day today, remember that Jesus is truly God with you. He wants to comfort you and bring you peace. He wants to lead and guide you through your day. He wants to bring you hope and purpose. He is there with you always, and His promises for you are yes and amen. You've just got to let Him in and partake of that relationship with Him.

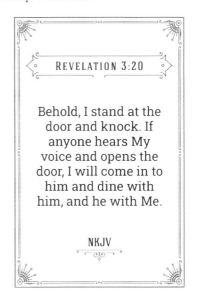

REVELATION 3:20

Behold, I stand at the door and knock. If anyone hears My voice and opens the door, I will come in to him and dine with him, and he with Me.

NKJV

Open the door and let Him in, and you can dine with Him, and partake with Him. And when you partake of the Divine nature, you begin to realize that you have a hope, even here and now, that is greater than any circumstance you may face.

EVERY SPIRITUAL BLESSING

As we explored last week, the Advent season of expectant longing for our future hope points us to the second coming of Jesus, and the fact that He will set right all the wrongs in this broken world. But Advent is also a reflection on the fact that Jesus has already come, and His coming has already set right much of what was wrong in our world.

The primary wrong He has righted is our separation from God, because of sin. We were hopeless sinners, cut off from the Holy God. We were unable to fulfill our created purpose, which is to glorify God, and were consequently heading towards a hopeless, meaningless life, followed by death and eternal damnation. The birth, death, and resurrection of Jesus has righted all of this. It righted it positionally for us, meaning those who have placed their faith in Jesus have been made right with God, and are granted eternal life and hope in Jesus. It also righted it practically, in that you and I, even though sinners, have been restored to relationship with God. Because we have been restored through Jesus, we are now heirs of the promise of God *(Gal. 3:29, Col. 3:24, Eph. 1:11)*. Much of that inheritance is yet to come, but much of it is also ours here and now. Here is what Paul has to say about this inheritance we have received:

Ephesians 1:3 (NKJV)
Blessed be the God and Father of our Lord Jesus Christ, who has
blessed us with every spiritual blessing in the heavenly places
in Christ.

In honesty, when I first read that verse, it just sounded like
religious speak. A platitude meant to sound nice. But after
reading it, and re-reading it, and re-reading it, I have found
that there is a depth of blessing and inheritance there that
I don't believe we have even begun to explore as Christians.
Pause for a moment and read that verse again... slowly... intentionally.

God has (past-tense) in Christ blessed us with every spiritual
blessing in the heavenly places. What this means is that every
spiritual blessing that is even possible has been given and
made available to you. There is no spiritual blessing that is not
yours for the taking. Peace that passes understanding? Yours.
Hope that defies reason? Yours. Patience in the face of trying
circumstances? Yours. Love that fills and overflows your soul?
Yours. These, and countless other Spiritual blessings have
already been made available to you through the miracle of
Christ's coming, which we celebrate at Advent.

How do we grab hold of these? By faith. The Holy Spirit
imparts these incredible blessings to us as we walk by faith,
trusting that they are ours. Whatever your spiritual need is
today, trust that God has provided for it through the cross, by
way of the manger. He has given it to you by the Holy Spirit.
Your job is simply to walk it out in faith.

DAY 10

THE BLESSING OF HIS LOVE

Advent celebrates the coming of the one Who is Immanuel, God with us. The past couple of days we have been exploring not only the future hope, but the present blessing that is ours because God is "with us". We have exceedingly great and precious promises *(2 Peter 1:4)* that are ours because Jesus was born, lived, died, and rose again as "God with us". We have every spiritual blessing available to us.

One of the very best spiritual blessings that Advent has made available to us is found in the simplicity of knowing God and His incredible love for us. What could we possibly have done to be so loved by the One we have so wronged? Nothing. There is nothing we could do, or have done. In fact, we have done everything possible to be unlovable. He loves us freely of His own will. Not because of what we have done, but because of Who He is.

His great love for you and me moved Him to forsake His glory and majesty, and put on swaddling blankets in a dirty stable feeding trough. Have you ever seen an animal's feeding trough? They are not exactly the picture of cleanliness. His great love for you and me moved Him to live 30+ years enduring the ache of a fallen creation. And while He did, He patiently loved and served those who would ultimately yell out "crucify Him!"

His great love for you and me moved Him to humble Himself, and to allow men who He could have wiped out with a word, to murder Him without cause. And His love for you and me moved Him to rise from the dead, so that not only can we be forgiven of our sin through His death, we can be given new life through His resurrection.

How great is His love for me! It is a worthwhile pursuit to spend my time, energy and effort to explore the depths of this love. To dig deep and to mine the depths of this love is a high calling. The further I dive into His love, the more I experience the other spiritual blessings He has given. The more that I know God's love, the more I can experience peace in the face of trial. The more that I know God's love, the more I can experience joy in the face of loss. The more that I know God's love, the more I can experience hope in the face of a hopeless world. This is what Paul was referring to in His prayer for us in Ephesians chapter 3.

Ephesians 3:18-19 (ESV)
May have strength to comprehend with all the saints what is the breadth and length and height and depth, and to know the love of Christ that surpasses knowledge, that you may be filled with all the fullness of God.

What a glorious and blessed calling we have been given to spend our lives exploring the width and length and height and depth of the love of Jesus. And the most amazing thing about it is this: because Jesus is God with us, when we spend our energy seeking out His love, the Bible tells us we are "filled with all the fullness of God". I cannot even comprehend that statement, but according to this scripture I can experience it. I want that. How about you?

Take a few minutes today and meditate on the great love of Jesus for you. Explore its width, dig into its depth, look up to its heights. As you do, allow God's grace to wash over you.

DAY 11

FILLED WITH THE FULLNESS

This week we have been discussing the many blessings that are ours because Jesus became "God with us." The Advent season is a reminder that the coming of Jesus not only separates us from our sins, and gives us a future and eternal hope, it also gives us hope today with the very presence of God in our daily lives. Because of Advent, Jesus is truly Immanuel, God with us. Yesterday we looked at *Ephesians 3:18–19*.

Ephesians 3:18–19 (ESV)
May have strength to comprehend with all the saints what is the breadth and length and height and depth, and to know the love of Christ that surpasses knowledge, that you may be filled with all the fullness of God.

In this passage we learned that when we spend our time, energy, and efforts exploring the love of Jesus, we can be "filled with all the fullness of God." What exactly does that mean? I don't know! I really don't know, and I'll show you why that's the case.

Verse 19 says that this love of Christ "surpasses knowledge", which means it cannot be known. The Greek word used for knowledge in that verse means "to know factually, or to be able to conceive it in the mind". It is a "head-knowledge."

Yet, the very same verse says that we can "know" the love of Christ that surpasses "knowledge." How does this work? Well, it's hard to catch it in our language, but if you knew Greek, you would get Paul's use of a play on words. The type of "knowing" he's talking about is not head-knowledge. The word used for "know" at the beginning of verse 19 means: "to know intimately, to feel, to perceive or experience". It is an experiential knowledge, and not a head-knowledge.

OK, I'm sorry if I am confusing you here, but this is important, so hang with me. What Paul is saying is this: Jesus' love for us, and His presence with us, through the Holy Spirit, is beyond our ability to "understand." Yet, we can intimately feel and experience it, and as we do we are filled with all of His fullness. In other words, you don't get to know how it works, but you can experience it.

What He's describing for us is the working of the gift of the Holy Spirit in our lives. This is possibly the greatest spiritual blessing that we receive because of Advent. You see, if "God with us" is only a reference to the birth and life of Jesus, then we don't actually have all that much to celebrate at Advent, because He is not physically here anymore. However, it

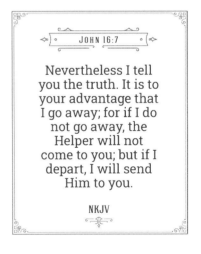

JOHN 16:7

Nevertheless I tell you the truth. It is to your advantage that I go away; for if I do not go away, the Helper will not come to you; but if I depart, I will send Him to you.

NKJV

means much more than that. It means that because Jesus was born and died and rose again, God is with us even now in a way that is much better than if we had the physical presence of Jesus on the earth. God is with us, and He is IN US. And because of this, we can be filled with all the fullness of God. What does this mean for you? We will talk more about that tomorrow.

DAY 12

GOD IN US

As we celebrate the coming of Jesus at Advent, we remember the long season of waiting that the Jewish people endured, longing with hopeful anticipation for their coming Messiah. They had their eyes and hopes set on the one who would be Immanuel, God with us. This week we have been looking at what the fulfillment of this prophecy in Jesus means for us, not only for our future hope, but in our present circumstances.

Yesterday we saw that because Jesus was born and died and rose again, God is with us now in a way that is much better than if we had the physical presence of Jesus on the earth. Jesus said so Himself in *John 16:7*.

This doesn't always add up for me, as I often feel like things would be much better if I had Jesus physically with me in my circumstances. What would it be like to have Jesus walk with me through my day? How great would it be to sit down with Him and talk through my problems and have him literally speak to me, and encourage me? How amazing would it be to see Him work miraculously in some trial or hardship I face, and audibly tell the wind and waves to be still?

Yet Jesus said "it is best for you that I go away." Why? Why was it best for him to go away? Doesn't His name, Immanuel, mean He will be WITH us? Jesus said "Because if I don't, the Helper won't come", and "But, if I do go away, then I will send Him to you." When Jesus said all of this to His disciples in John 16, they must have been confused, just as I am sometimes. But not long after that they got it, and it suddenly made sense. You see, because Jesus ascended to Heaven, He sent us the Holy Spirit to not only be "God with us", but God IN US. This is quite possibly the best current blessing we have access to because of Advent!

Unfortunately, many Christians, myself included at times, do not take full advantage of this blessing. As a believer in Jesus, the Holy Spirit lives inside of me. He is with me and He is in me. His title is the Greek word "Paraclete", which means: comforter, encourager, counselor, or advocate. You see, the Holy Spirit is the one Who imparts to me all of the spiritual blessings I receive. He is the source of my hope, joy, peace, love, and any other spiritual fruit I may see in my life *(Galatians 5:22-25)*. Jesus said that the Spirit will teach us all things, and remind us of the things we have learned from Him *(John 16:13-14)*. He is the one Who speaks to me and gives me guidance and direction in my life. He is the one Who gives me the power and strength I need to live this Christian life. But this is just the tip of the iceberg.

Through my relationship with Him, He not only meets my spiritual and emotional needs, but I can have such an abundance in Him that these same spiritual blessings flow out of my life like a rushing river onto those around me.

Take a moment to thank the Holy Spirit for His presence in your life that has been made possible by Advent. And as you do, do something for me - just try it...ask God for more. Ask Him for a keener awareness of the Holy Spirit's presence and work in your life. Ask Him for the outworking of the Spiritual Gifts in your life. Ask Him for more of the blessing and fruit of the Spirit. Ask Him for more in your relationship with the Holy Spirit. Ask Him for the rivers of living water He promised. Jesus has said that this is a prayer God loves to answer *(Luke 11:13)*.

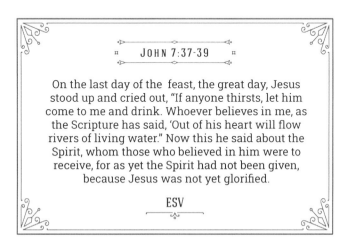

JOHN 7:37-39

On the last day of the feast, the great day, Jesus stood up and cried out, "If anyone thirsts, let him come to me and drink. Whoever believes in me, as the Scripture has said, 'Out of his heart will flow rivers of living water." Now this he said about the Spirit, whom those who believed in him were to receive, for as yet the Spirit had not been given, because Jesus was not yet glorified.

ESV

JUST AN APPETIZER

Congratulations, you are halfway through our Advent journey! Stick with it, as I believe God has a blessing in store for you as you commit to finish strong.

You may be wondering how all this talk of current blessing and spiritual abundance the past few days ties together with the Ache of Advent we discussed last week. The blessing of God does not remove the ache, groaning, and longing for the wrongs in this world to be made right, but if anything, it actually amplifies them.

The incredible blessings of God's peace, presence, and power in my life today highlights the sharp relief of how far our world is from experiencing the perfection that God has in store. It is a foretaste of the future glory that will be ours in eternity, the magnitude of which we cannot even imagine. Look with me at how Paul describes it.

1 Corinthians 2:9 (NKJV)
But as it is written: "Eye has not seen, nor ear heard, Nor have entered into the heart of man The things which God has prepared for those who love Him."

In other words, you can't even imagine how good God's plans

are for you in His future Kingdom, and eventually in the new heaven and earth He will make. The blessing and power and life in the Spirit that we are able to experience here is just a small hint at that goodness to come. The spiritual blessings you and I can receive today are like an appetizer, or a teaser to keep our eyes on the prize of our True Country. It's as if God is saying to us, "I know that this world is hard, but just hang on, as I've got good things coming!"

It's a little like eating out at a restaurant, and noticing that the waiter is walking by with the dessert tray. You peek over and see various dishes composed of scrumptious chocolate, caramel, raspberry compote, creme brûlée, and your mouth just can't help but water at the thought of how good they must all taste. This is the heart behind the Advent celebration; a picture of the Holy ache that we not only can, but should have for our true home. We must never feel too much at home, too comfortable, or too much at ease here.

Let your mouth water for what's coming. Let your hopes rise at the thought of the goodness of Heaven and your true home. Let the taste of God's blessings that you receive here and now stir your heart with longing, and with a fire in your bones to live for what God will bring as He makes all things new.

Revelation 21:3-4 (NLT)
I heard a loud shout from the throne, saying, "Look, God's home is now among his people! He will live with them, and they will be his people. God himself will be with them. He will wipe every tear from their eyes, and there will be no more death or sorrow or crying or pain. All these things are gone forever."

DAY 14

THE SPIRIT GROANS WITH US

As we have seen, the beauty of Advent is that because of the coming of Jesus, God is indeed with us and in us. And just as the Israelites awaited their coming messiah, we now await the day that God will not only be with us, but we will be with Him. As Revelation 21 says, God's home will be among His people. All of the death, sorrow and pain in this world will be gone forever.

Even as our hopes and hearts are set on that glory to be revealed to us, sometimes it all seems to be too much in the here and now. Sometimes circumstances and hardships seem to eclipse that future hope, and all you can do is fall apart. There are times in my life when I can't even seem to pray because I simply have no words to express.

This is where the incredible blessing of the Holy Spirit's presence in our lives really shows. In those times, even if all we can do is fall apart, we can fall apart in His arms. We don't have to know what to say. We don't have to know what to pray. Because He is WITH US, and especially because He is IN US, we can cast ourselves fully on Him, and ask Him to intervene on our behalf.

Look with me at this encouragement from Romans 8:26.

ROMANS 8:26

Likewise the Spirit helps us in our
weakness. For we do not know what to
pray for as we ought, but the Spirit himself
intercedes for us with groanings too deep
for words.

ESV

When we are weak, He is strong. In fact, when all I can do is sigh, and the last thing I have to give is a whimper or a sob, that's when He steps in and intercedes for me. He hears my heart and He aches with me. He hears those things I simply cannot put into words, and He brings them before God's throne, even when I can't. That is how WITH US He is.

This is why *1 Peter 5:7* says to *"cast all your anxieties on Him, because He cares for you."* When those unbearable burdens, fears, and anxieties rise up, and the weight of the world seems too much, I can simply come to Him and exchange my stress and fears for the peace that surpasses understanding *(Philippians 4:6-7)*.

Whatever you face today, know that God is with you. He is interceding for you, even when you don't have the words. He is working on your behalf, and He knows what you need - even when you don't. Cast yourself on Him. Let it all go, and let Him step in.

DAY 15

WHILE YOU'RE WAITING, HE'S WORKING

It's only 10 days til Christmas! Some of you may be like me, and have not finished all your shopping yet, and might be stressing out a little. Or if you weren't stressing out before you read this, now you are. Maybe you are not big on Christmas and are just ready for it to all be over. Or perhaps you are one of those who wish we could have another month of celebration. Or maybe, like most kids at this point, you just can't wait for it to come. The anticipation is growing and growing.

The Jewish people waited for their messiah for generations. We could look at early scriptures and say that they waited for thousands of years. But let's be conservative and say that they only really knew they needed a messiah by the mouths of the prophets, which means that they waited for over 700 years for Him to come. At day 15 we are almost 2/3rds through Advent this year, which could be compared to Israel's having waited 420 of 700 years before the Messiah appeared.

In the first 300 years of that waiting God spoke through the prophets by the Holy Spirit. He gave the people message after message of encouragement about the hope they had in the coming messiah. Then, after about 300 years, the Holy Spirit stopped speaking. There was no prophetic voice. There were no new revelations or encouragements from God.

In fact, there is no Biblical record of what happened between the last of the prophets and the birth of Jesus. We have secular and apocryphal history, but no inspired record of God's voice, and interaction with His people.

Imagine living in that 400 year period of waiting. You might be wondering if God had forgotten about you. Was He going to keep His promise to bring a messiah? Was that just an old legend that your grandparents believed in?

What we don't see in scripture, we do see in history. While Israel was waiting, God was working. He was working behind the scenes on their behalf the entire time. He was establishing empires and trade routes, He was ushering in favorable circumstances for the message of the kingdom to travel freely throughout the known world, He was preparing hearts and minds. He knew the timeline, even if they didn't, and He was going to make it happen.

Isaiah 64:4 (NIV)
Since ancient times no one has heard, no ear has perceived, no eye has seen any God besides you, who acts on behalf of those who wait for him.

God works for those who wait on Him. While Israel was waiting, God was working. The same thing is true for you. We're all in a celebratory Advent season of waiting for Christmas, but maybe you're also in a difficult season of waiting in your personal life. Maybe you feel a little like the Israelites did during those 400 years of silence. You're wondering where God is, and if He has really heard your prayers. You wonder if He really cares about you, and if He is going to be true to His Word. Remember, while you're waiting, He's working.

Psalm 130:5 (NKJV)
I wait for the Lord, my soul waits, And in His word I do hope.

DAY 16

ANTICIPATION BUILDS

As we get closer and closer to Christmas my kids are getting more and more excited about it. They are searching online for presents for each other, thinking about all of the fun festivities, and singing Christmas songs as they walk around the house.

This reminds me that the anticipation of the Jews grew greater and greater as the birth of Christ approached. You may not realize this, but most Jewish scholars in Jesus' day anticipated the Messiah to arrive at any time. We don't often think about this because we know that they ultimately rejected him. They thought He would be a political savior, restoring the earthly kingdom of Israel, but He came to be a total savior, restoring mankind to Himself, and establishing the Kingdom of Heaven. However, they knew from multiple prophecies, the clearest being found in Daniel chapter 9, that the Messiah should come in their generation. Imagine the constant state of excitement they must have lived in! With each new rising spiritual or political leader they must have asked "could this be the one?" They would have begun to live their lives in anticipation of His coming.

Our reminder of their waiting through Advent is a picture of our waiting for Christ's second coming. As I think about the anticipation the Jews must have had, I am beginning to realize that this is the same anticipation we should have as we look toward the day of full salvation - the Day of the Lord. What joy will be ours when we finally see our Savior face to face! Imagine the huge party we're going to have at the wedding feast of the Lamb, as He rights all the wrongs, and ushers in eternal peace. This anticipation should not only bring joy and expectancy to our hearts about the future, it should also transform our lives today!

2 Peter 3:11-12 (NKJV)
11 Therefore, since all these things will be dissolved, what manner of persons ought you to be in holy conduct and godliness, 12 looking for and hastening the coming of the day of God, because of which the heavens will be dissolved, being on fire, and the elements will melt with fervent heat?

If we live in anticipation of Jesus' coming, with our hope set on Heaven and eternity, then our lives will look different than if we are just living for the here and now. When I live for the here and now I have little reason for hope. As we have already discussed thoroughly, this world is not a hopeful place apart from Jesus. There is so much evil and pain and heartache and loss. If my heart's focus is on attaining earthly goals, and reaching the "American Dream", ultimately I will be disappointed. But if I let me heart soar at the thought of the incredible goodness of God's plan, and let my anticipation and expectancy of His arrival drive my earthly priorities and goals, then my life will be full of joy and peace and hope, no matter what circumstances I may face.

So let the anticipation build, and let your heart long for and get excited about the day that is coming. It's closer than it's ever been, and it's more important now than ever before to let our lives reflect that excitement. Our eternal Christmas morning is coming, and all the goodness that comes with it...I for one cannot wait to see what's waiting for me under the tree.

AS HE IS WITH US, WE ARE WITH THEM

The Advent celebration centers on the fact that Jesus is Immanuel, God with us. We have discussed many different ways in which He is with us, and there is incredible blessing to be found in the truth that God is with us. As we grasp this truth, our eyes naturally begin to focus on the eternal, rather than the temporal. We begin to have a heavenly focus.

One way this heavenly focus should work itself out in our lives is that we begin to realize that in the same way Jesus is "God with us", we are to be "with" others. You and I are the only Bible many people will read. You and I are the closest many people will come to meeting Jesus. We are His representatives here on earth. We have been sent here on a mission. Yes, we may long for our True Country, and we should live with our eyes set on the Kingdom of Heaven, but the way that works itself out here and now is that we should live as if we are here on a mission from our King.

All the things you worry about now will be gone before you know it, and you will be sitting at Jesus' feet, worshipping and basking in His glory for eternity, with no more tears, no more depression, and no more fear! But there are many people that you know, and regularly interact with, who do not have this same hope. And without this hope in Jesus those people will spend eternity separated from God, and separated from you. This is why Paul tells us to "Make the most of every opportunity in these evil days." *(Ephesians 5:16 NLT)* We are not here for ourselves. If this life were about me, it would actually be far better for me to go and be with Jesus. Paul the apostle felt the same way *(read Philippians 1:23-25)*. The reason I am still here is to represent Jesus to those who don't yet know His great love. I am here to be "with them" the same way that Jesus is with me. My life, my actions, my words, should all point people towards the hope that I have in Him.

My prayer is that as I am "with people" they will sense that God is with me, and that He will draw them to Himself through my lifestyle, words, and actions that are lived in worship to Him. Jesus said "if I be lifted up, I will draw all men to myself" *(John 12:32)*. I believe that, so I want my life to lift up Jesus. Look at what Jesus had to say about this:

Matthew 5:14-16 (NKJV)
"You are the light of the world. A city that is set on a hill cannot be hidden. Nor do they light a lamp and put it under a basket, but on a lampstand, and it gives light to all who are in the house. Let your light so shine before men, that they may see your good works and glorify your Father in heaven."

As Christmas draws near it is important think and pray about who the Lord has placed in your sphere of influence. Who Has God placed in your life, and how would He have you love them with the love of Jesus? How would God have you be "with" them?

Take a few minutes right now and pray. Ask God to reveal those people to you. Write their names down on a sheet of paper, or in a note on your phone. Then pray and think about how you can be with them as Jesus is with you. Start a conversation about spiritual things with them. Invite them to church for Christmas. I realize it's scary, but when you tell someone about Jesus, you are literally telling them the best news they will ever hear. Don't worry, God will be with you.

DAY 18

SHARING THE JOY

As we close in on Christmas week, people around us have started to hustle & bustle, busily taking care of whatever business they have before they take time off for the holiday. Many people are working overtime to make ends meet for Christmas, while others are scrambling for last minute gifts or preparations. There is an excitement in the air as Christmas approaches.

At the same time, in the midst of the hustle and bustle, there is an associated rise in stress, anxiety, depression, and loneliness. Many people face the Christmas season with seemingly opposite feelings of what it should bring. A large part of this is because Christmas, as it is typically celebrated, does not actually celebrate Jesus at all. It celebrates gifts, food, family, & the coming of winter. None of those things are bad in themselves, but if your life doesn't check all the right boxes for a "Merry Christmas", then there's not really much to celebrate. Even if it does, if those things are all that you celebrated, then you are left with a bit of an empty feeling when Christmas Day is over.

This is a challenge for us as Christians, in keeping our focus. It is difficult to not be distracted by the craziness and worldly focus on secondary things, and to keep our eyes on what we are really celebrating. What we have is "good news of great joy for ALL people" *(Luke 2:10)*, which is not just for those who have families, not just for those who can afford gifts and nice meals, and not just for those who love the coming of winter and all its trappings.

As followers of Jesus, we know the true joy that Christmas brings. The Savior has come, our Messiah is here, and His coming is a blessing to everyone! We were in darkness, and now we have light. Isaiah put this very well as he prophetically anticipated Jesus' coming.

ISAIAH 9:2

The people who walked in darkness
Have seen a great light;
Those who dwelt in the land of the
shadow of death,

NKJV

Jesus has shined that light on us. We no longer walk in darkness, as we are children of the light. This is what and why we celebrate. And now that this light has shone in our hearts, we have been given the privilege and blessing of shining it on others.

Remember as you go through the hustle and bustle of this season that you are a light-bearer. You get to shine the true meaning of Christmas into each and every situation you enter. How can you shine the hope and light and love of Jesus with those in your path?

How can you shine the true light of Christmas on those who are caught up in the hustle & bustle of the season, or those who are dealing with stress, anxiety, depression, or loneliness?

Maybe it's as simple as buying the person in line behind you coffee at Starbucks. Maybe it's asking the checker at the grocery how they are doing, and taking a real interest in them. Maybe it's inviting that single person you know to join your family for Christmas. And as you do those things, make the most of the opportunities that come up. Take the chance to be a kingdom-representative. Take the chance of inviting that person to Christmas Eve services at your church. And as the opportunity to share Jesus comes up (because it will), do it! Share that He has loved and blessed you so much that you just wanted to spread that joy to others.

2 Corinthians 4:6 (NKJV)
For it is the God who commanded light to shine out of darkness, who has shone in our hearts to give the light of the knowledge of the glory of God in the face of Jesus Christ.

A MESSY FAMILY TREE

We are now 7 days from Christmas! We are in the home stretch, the final week. As we enter this final countdown to our celebrations of Jesus' birth, I want to take a few days to look at the people and events leading up to, and immediately after the birth of Christ, and how they relate to our celebration of Advent.

Let's start with Jesus' Family tree. The Jewish people in Jesus' day were meticulous record keepers, and most Jews could trace their lineage back many generations. This was important for Jesus, because the Messiah must sit on the throne of David, King of Israel, which meant He must be a descendant of King David. We see the genealogy of Jesus listed in two places in scripture - Matthew 1 and Luke 3. Now, if you go and read these two side by side, you will see they are different. Wait a second, how can they be different? Well, if you've ever looked up your family tree on Ancestry.com, you know that you have two different branches of your family history; your mothers' side and your fathers' side.

Most scholars believe that the two genealogies we see presented in scripture are: 1. The legal genealogy of Jesus through Joseph, His adopted father, and 2. His blood genealogy through Mary, His mother. The amazing thing is that Jesus can lay a legal claim to the throne of David through either genealogy! He was a descendant of David both through blood and adoption! But the most amazing thing about Jesus' genealogies is not so much in His ability to claim the throne, but in the people who were a part of His family tree.

In Jesus' day, it was typical to use the male head's of house as the title-bearers in a given genealogy. Rarely were women ever mentioned in a genealogy. Yet, in the genealogy of Jesus there are four women mentioned by name. And these women were probably not the kind of people you would want to admit as being in your family tree. This was especially as a Jew, or one seeking to claim a Royal throne.

The first woman mentioned is Tamar, the daughter-in-law of Judah. Tamar's husband died, and she tricked her father-in-law into sleeping with her in order to get pregnant so she could have a child. Sounds like daytime TV doesn't it? The second is Rahab, the woman who hid the spies of Israel in Jericho as they prepared to take the land. Rahab was not a Jew, she was a Canaanite. Not only that, she was a prostitute. Not exactly your model family member. The third is Ruth, perhaps the only truly honorable one out of the group. Yet, she was also a foreigner, as she was a Moabite. The Moabites were under a curse from God because they turned their backs on Israel. The fourth woman in His genealogy was Bathsheba, who apparently was so looked down upon that she wasn't worth mentioning by name, and Matthew's genealogy listed her as "the wife of Uriah". Bathsheba was the woman King David had an affair with. He ultimately ended up killing her husband, so he could cover up her pregnancy and have her for himself. And you thought your family had problems! Now, there are many more names and many more stories in His genealogies, but these four women exemplify God's amazing grace, and the beauty of His plan for redeeming and uniting mankind through the coming of the Messiah.

God broke down many barriers in the lineage of Jesus. He broke down racial/ethnic barriers by including nations outside the covenant in His heritage. He broke down gender barriers and made all people equal in Him. He broke down sin barriers in that He included many shady characters in His family tree. God demonstrated, before Jesus was even born, how vast and unconditional His love is by redeeming the stories of countless sinful and broken individuals, and showing them worth and honor by bringing the Messiah through their lineage. He put on full display His love for all mankind, and that He wants all people to come to Him (*1 Timothy 2:4*).

Here's how this relates to you and me. Because of the Advent of the Messiah, you and I and our messy stories are welcome in the family of God. Whatever your past, whatever your family history, whatever your own sinful tendencies, you are welcome in God's family. Perhaps this has not been the case for you in this world. Perhaps either because of your race, your gender, your actions, your inaction, your looks, or simply because people don't seem to like you, you feel like an outsider. You feel like you are second-class. You feel like you don't fit in, and aren't part of the cool crowd, or the in-group. Well, let me tell you that there are no second-class citizens in God's kingdom, and in His family. You are welcome, you are loved, you are received. Rest in that, celebrate it, and know that you are a child who is loved by your God.

Galatians 3:28 (NKJV)
There is neither Jew nor Greek, there is neither slave nor free, there is neither male nor female; for you are all one in Christ Jesus.

COURAGEOUS FAITH

There is one woman in Jesus' line who we are all familiar with, that I didn't mention yesterday. She is Mary, the mother of Jesus.

There are varied thoughts and traditions surrounding Mary. For our purposes I'd like to just focus on what the Bible, and the cultural context of Jesus' day tell us about who she might have been. Mary was engaged to be married, which was almost certainly a prearranged marriage, according to the custom of the day. The fact that she wasn't yet married when we meet her means that she was probably still very young. In that time girls would usually be married within 1-2 years of reaching puberty. So Mary was likely around 14 years old when we meet her in Luke 1. If you'd like more context for our study, now would be a good time to take a few minutes and read *Luke 1:26-38*.

Now, I want you to imagine what it would have been like to be Mary in this situation. An angel shows up and declares that you are pregnant, even though you are a virgin, and that your son will be the Messiah. You'd have countless thoughts swirling through your mind. For starters, you are a Jewish girl, and you have been awaiting the coming of the messiah. What excitement it must have brought to know that He is coming, but to then think that you would be privileged enough to be His mother! Words would not be enough to express the joy you must have felt at this privilege. On the other hand, what would Joseph think? What would your parents think? What would your friends and neighbors think? Who would possibly believe you? It's too far-fetched! This would change your life. All of your prior plans and hopes would now have to be re-oriented around this interruption. And as much as it would be a blessing to bear the messiah, all of the fallout from the circumstances of His birth could potentially label you as an immoral woman, a fornicator.

Mary was "blessed and highly favored among women" *(Luke 1:28)*, yet she had to live with the perceived shame of conceiving a child out of wedlock. She had to live as walking by faith, even when those around her may not have believed her report. On the contrary, most people probably believed the worst about her. Sometimes fulfillment of God's promises, and answers to our prayers come in packages that we don't expect. As miraculous and amazing as His blessings and answers to prayer are, they may still come with their own share of difficulties and hardships. Mary inevitably faced ridicule, judgment, and condemnation. This on top of the challenge of surrendering her own plans for her life.

The same will be true for you and me if we desire to see God's promises come to fruition in our lives, and long for the coming of His Kingdom. Jesus has called us to live a life that is re-oriented around the fact that He has come, and is coming again. He has called us to walk by faith, accepting the commission He has for us to be His ambassadors. As Mary literally carried Him into the world, we are to carry Him with us as we bear the message of Jesus into the world. The amazing blessings of promises fulfilled, and the beauty of answered prayers are well worth the cost.

Thankfully, God knew what He was doing, and He chose a girl

who was up to the challenge. Mary's answer to the angel was simple, bold, faith-filled, and courageous. She said, "I am the lord's servant, may your word to me be fulfilled". So simple, and yet so profound.

May we have the same bold and courageous faith as the Lord asks us to trust His promises. May we walk boldly in faith as we carry Jesus into a world that desperately needs Him.

JOSHUA 1:9

Have I not commanded you? Be strong and of good courage; do not be afraid, nor be dismayed, for the Lord your God is with you wherever you go.

NKJV

DAY 21

SAYING YES TO GOD

One of the people that was very much involved in Jesus' birth and early life is Joseph. Joseph was Mary's husband, and Jesus' stepfather. We don't hear or talk all that much about Joseph, which is a shame. We don't know much about Joseph, but what we do know from the scriptures speaks loudly about his character and devotion. If you'd like some better context for our study, read *Matthew 1:18-25 & Matthew 2:13-23*. When we first meet Joseph, he is engaged to Mary. He finds out that she is pregnant with a child that is not his, and he is, of course, heart-broken. In Joseph's day, Mary could have been publicly shunned, or even put to death for this breach of trust. But Joseph is a kind and gentle man, so he doesn't want to put her through the public shame & disgrace of taking her to the courts, which he could have done. Instead, he decides he's going to break the engagement quietly, and let her alone. Joseph is thinking this all through when an angel appears to him in a dream, and tells him that her pregnancy was of God, and that she was bearing the Messiah.

I want you to imagine yourself as Joseph for a moment. You are heartbroken and humiliated because of this whole situation. You could really stick it to her by publicly shaming her, but you just can't bring yourself to do that, so you humbly choose to walk away. Then you have this incredible dream where an angel tells you that Mary did not cheat on you, but that the baby she is carrying is the Messiah, and you are to proceed with marrying her. How would you feel when you woke up in the morning? If it were me, I would have had lots of questions. Was that dream real? Am I crazy? Am I just imagining things? If I marry her, everyone will think the baby is mine, and then she and I will both bear the shame of having a child before marriage.

This would have been difficult for Joseph to obey. He was giving up a lot to follow what the angel said. People would talk about them. People would judge them. They would be marked by this for life. He would have to help raise a child that was not his in the true sense. Not to mention the possibility that his dream was not actually an angel at all, but was just a dream. I would have been tempted to just brush off the dream and move on with my life.

But what did Joseph do? When he woke up, he did as the Lord commanded him and took Mary as his wife *(Matthew 1:24)*. Joseph walked in simple faith and obedience to God. Why? Because he believed God. Joseph was not an extraordinary man, as he was just a simple builder. But this ordinary man had an extraordinary faith in God. He trusted God, and so when God said to do something, he did it. We see this time and again in Matthew 1 & 2. Joseph repeatedly received dreams from God, and he just kept saying "yes" to what God told him to do, moving his family around multiple times in obedience to God. Joseph's simple faith and obedience in saying "yes" to God repeatedly protected the newborn Messiah from the hands of those who would seek to kill him. His simple "yes" brought Jesus through multiple circumstances as a young child that fulfilled prophecies given about Him over 700 years before.

I want to be like Joseph, and the great thing is that I can be.

You see, Joseph was not a theologian, He was not an evangelist, He was not a holy roller. He was just a simple man who said "yes" to God. We can all do that. No matter your talent, ability, weakness, fear, struggle, or doubt, you can say "yes" to God. And let me tell you, that is what He is looking for.

2 Chronicles 16:9a (NKJV)
For the eyes of the Lord run to and fro throughout the whole earth, to show Himself strong on behalf of those whose heart is loyal to Him.

God is looking for men and women who will say "yes" to Him. He's looking for people who will believe Him, believe His promises, and say "yes" to what He asks in light of those promises. As you celebrate Advent, and long for the promises of God in your life, can you be one who will say "yes" to God? You might be wondering what the question is that you are saying yes to, however, you may not get to know that yet. But are you willing to say "Yes", no matter the question? If you can bring yourself to that point, God is just waiting to show Himself strong on your behalf.

Take a moment today and be honest with yourself about whether you are willing to say "yes" to whatever God may ask of you. If not, ask God to help you change your heart towards Him. If you are willing, ask Him for an opportunity to practice your "Yes".

PROVERBS 3:5-6

Trust in the Lord with all your heart;
do not depend on your own understanding.
Seek his will in all you do, and he will show
you which path to take.

NLT

DAY 22

THE PINNACLE OF LIFE

There is a little-known man who we only hear about one time in Scripture, right after the birth of Jesus. His name was Simeon. For context, you can read *Luke 2:25-35*. Simeon was nobody really special, except for his steadfast hope and trust in God. Simeon was simply a man who was waiting for the Messiah. Luke tells us that the Holy Spirit was upon him, and had told him that he would not die before he saw the Lord's Messiah. What incredible hope that must have brought to Simeon. As we've discussed, the Jews had been waiting for 700 years for the coming of the Messiah, and in the last 400 years they had not heard much of anything from God on the subject. But Simeon heard from God, and He told him that "The messiah is coming, and you are going to meet Him".

When we meet Simeon in Luke 2 he is in the temple, and upon seeing the baby Jesus with His parents, he immediately takes Jesus in his arms and starts praising God. In that moment of praise he says "Lord, you can take me home now, for I have seen Your salvation!"

Simeon's entire hope for his life was bound up in the coming of the Messiah. He lived with such expectant hope, that once he met Him he was complete, and ready to go home to the Lord. When I think of people with such simplicity of heart, and great hope in God, I realize how unimportant and trivial so many of my pursuits in life are. There are many things that I think are so important, but which have no real eternal value at all. Simeon knew what really mattered. For him, having seen the Messiah was enough. Nothing in life could ever top that moment, and he was ready to go home.

The actor/comedian Jim Carrey, who is not a believer to my knowledge, made an interesting statement a few years back. He said "I think everybody should get rich and famous and do everything they ever dreamed of so they can see that it's not the answer." Now, if I say something like that it doesn't hold much value, because I'm not rich and famous, and I haven't done everything I ever dreamed of. But when someone like Jim Carrey says it, we need to pay attention. He has achieved incredible success and wealth, and gets to do basically whatever he wants. However, it seems he has realized that it leaves him empty inside. He has reached the pinnacle of life, as most people would define it, and says that there's nothing there when you get to the top.

Simeon knew that the most important, most life-giving thing he could do, was to spend his life in service and love to God, looking for the hope of the coming Messiah. He truly reached the pinnacle of existence, and in that moment of meeting the Messiah, God born as man, he knew he didn't need anything else.

May we recognize that the pinnacle of our existence is found in Him, and not in any achievement or goal we might have in this life. May we have the same simplicity of heart as Simeon, seeking only to see Jesus. Seeking only to find our life in relationship to Him, and longing for His coming.

2 Corinthians 4:18 (NKJV)
While we do not look at the things which are seen, but at the things which are not seen. For the things which are seen are temporary, but the things which are not seen are eternal.

DAY 23

WORTH THE WAIT

Another little-known person surrounding the birth of Christ was the prophetess Anna. You might be thinking, who is Anna? I've never heard of her! Exactly. Immediately after Simeon encountered the infant Jesus in the temple, we meet Anna.

Luke 2:36–38 (NKJV)
Now there was one, Anna, a prophetess, the daughter of
Phanuel, of the tribe of Asher. She was of a great age, and
had lived with a husband seven years from her virginity; and
this woman was a widow of about eighty–four years, who did
not depart from the temple, but served God with fastings and
prayers night and day. And coming in that instant she gave
thanks to the Lord, and spoke of Him to all those who looked for
redemption in Jerusalem.

Anna was likely widowed when she was around 21-22 years old. At the point we meet her, she had been a widow for over 60 years. As a widow in the first century, she had no means of providing for herself, and no hope of "success" in life, unless she re-married. For whatever reason, this didn't happen for Anna. So she decided to live her life completely and solely for the Lord. She was in the temple day and night, and was completely devoted to serving the Lord. A lot of people might have been frustrated with this lot in life, but Anna embraced her role and calling with great devotion and passion. She spent day and night before the Lord, ministering to the people in her role as a prophet.

The scriptures tell us that when Anna met Jesus, she gave thanks to God, and excitedly began to tell others about Him. The last 60 years of Anna's life had been spent waiting on the Lord. In this moment of meeting the newborn Messiah, she must have felt as if her 60 years of waiting on the Lord had finally come to fruition. The wait had been worth it. This is always true for the believer. The wait is always worth it. Throughout the scriptures we are encouraged to "wait on the Lord" *(Psalm 27:13-14, Lamentations 3:25, Isaiah 30:18, James 5:7-8, Micah 7:7, Psalm 37:34, Psalm 62:5* and many more). Waiting on the Lord is never a waste of time. Anna testifies to this, as does all of scripture.

In this season of Advent, we remember the waiting of the Jews for the coming Messiah, and we are currently waiting for the second coming of Jesus to set right the wrongs in this world. Whatever your current season of "waiting", whether waiting for resolution of a problem in your life, or fulfillment of a promise of the Lord, your wait is worth it. Your wait is not a

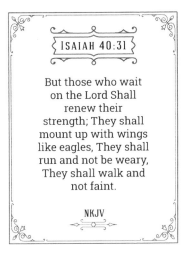

ISAIAH 40:31

But those who wait on the Lord Shall renew their strength; They shall mount up with wings like eagles, They shall run and not be weary, They shall walk and not faint.

NKJV

waste of time, and your season of waiting and trial is actually working on your behalf *(2 Corinthians 4:17)*.

Wait on the Lord, put your hope and trust in Him and His Word, and you will not be let down. He is worth the wait.

DAY 24

THE FINAL COUNTDOWN

It is Christmas Eve! Tomorrow we celebrate the fact that the Savior has come, love incarnate came down and met us in our mess. Today is the final countdown, and we are in the final minutes and hours before our celebrations begin. Kids around the world are looking under Christmas trees, while parents around the world scramble to wrap gifts and purchase last minute necessities. There is an excitement in the air, and also a little bit of stress as people remember, "Oh, I still need to do _____!"

Christmas doesn't only serve as a reminder of the fact that Jesus came and lived and died for us, but also as a reminder that He is coming again. Just as today is Christmas Eve, and we are in the final hours before Christmas, we are also living in the final days before Jesus' glorious return for His Church. We are in the "Christmas Eve" of the eternal calendar. I realize that sometimes it doesn't feel like that. It's been over 2,000 years since Jesus came the first time, and for us time drags on slowly. It's easy to wonder "Is he really coming back? It's been so long, how can we know?", yet the Holy Spirit anticipated these questions.

2 Peter 3:3-4 (ESV)
Knowing this first of all, that scoffers will come in the last days

with scoffing, following their own sinful desires. They will say, "Where is the promise of his coming? For ever since the fathers fell asleep, all things are continuing as they were from the beginning of creation."

But with each passing day our redemption draws nearer. Especially given current events, and the state of world affairs, I truly believe He may come for us at any moment. As I contemplate this fact, it has made me ask myself some reflective questions.

Am I really living my life as if Jesus is coming back for me tomorrow? Am I daily living my life today as if it is Christmas Eve, and I've got some preparations left to do before the great celebration tomorrow? Do my priorities reflect the fact that this world is fleeting, and I have the ability to make investments for eternity with my limited time here and now?

If I'm honest with myself, the answer to these questions is sometimes "no". My natural tendency is to choose temporal safety, earthly gain, quick satisfaction, and short-term happiness.

Looking at the parable of the ten virgins, the parable of the fig tree, the parable of the wise servant, and the parable of the talents *(Luke 21, Matthew 24–25)*, in each of these Jesus encourages us to get ready. It's Christmas Eve! Buy the last-minute gifts, make the last-minute preparations, make sure you're prepared for the big party.

We are in for an amazing blowout of truly epic proportions. A celebration the likes of which no created being has ever seen. You think you know how to throw a party or celebrate Christmas? Psh... right... compared to one thrown by the King of the Universe? You can't even imagine what he has in store.

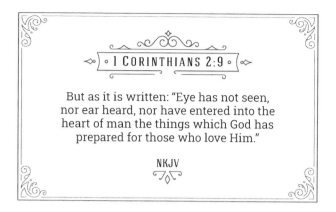

1 CORINTHIANS 2:9

But as it is written: "Eye has not seen,
nor ear heard, nor have entered into the
heart of man the things which God has
prepared for those who love Him."

NKJV

Let us be those who are READY for the party, and not like the
ones who were invited and got distracted with their day-to-
day business, who missed out on the wedding feast *(Matthew
22:1–10)*.

In what ways do you need to prepare for Jesus' coming? Do
you have some unfinished business in your heart with Him?
Do you need to re-align your life priorities with eternity in
view? What do you need to do to be ready for the big day?

ITS PARTY TIME

Luke 2:10-11 (NKJV)
Then the angel said to them, "Do not be afraid, for behold, I
bring you good tidings of great joy which will be to all people.
For there is born to you this day in the city of David a Savior,
who is Christ the Lord.

It is here, Christmas Day! The long-hoped-for Messiah has
come. The Hope of Israel is here, He is finally "God with Us".
The birth of Jesus in Bethlehem represents the beginning
of a new hope for mankind. Everything was broken before,
hopeless and destined for ruin. Because of Jesus, all can be
made new. The angels sang and rejoiced at the birth of Christ
because it ushered in a new future, not only for all mankind,
but also the entire universe. All of the mess and brokenness
caused by man, sin, and Satan will be remedied.

The birth of Jesus was the first step in the beautiful messianic
story of redemption for the universe. His humble life, death,
and resurrection paved the way for restored relationship
between man and God. Now you and I, sinners and deserving
of judgment, can have unhindered access to the throne room
of God through His grace, which bought for us at the cross
(Hebrews 4:16). We can receive love and grace and mercy to
help us in time of need. We can have a loving relationship,

which was before unavailable, with our Heavenly Father who desires good things for us *(Romans 8:32)*.

And this is just the beginning! The Birth of Jesus was the first sign of hope that foreshadows the time of the end, when our loving God will finally usher in His full reign over the earth, and our deepest longings and hopes as a people will finally be realized and fulfilled.

Fear not, there is born this day a savior, which is Christ the Lord. The waiting is finally over, our Hope has come, and He is coming again. It's time to celebrate!

Our Christmas gatherings are a foreshadowing of the great and glorious day that we awake into that eternal Christmas morning of not only having God with us, but actually being with Him. Let your celebrations today be full of joy and laughter and hope because of what Jesus has done, and what He will do. Let's practice today what it will be like to open that great gift of eternal life and enter into the full promise of God. What a day that will be!

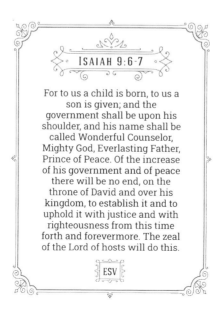

ISAIAH 9:6-7

For to us a child is born, to us a son is given; and the government shall be upon his shoulder, and his name shall be called Wonderful Counselor, Mighty God, Everlasting Father, Prince of Peace. Of the increase of his government and of peace there will be no end, on the throne of David and over his kingdom, to establish it and to uphold it with justice and with righteousness from this time forth and forevermore. The zeal of the Lord of hosts will do this.

ESV

EPILOGUE

Well, that's it, Christmas is over. What now? The after-Christmas letdown seems to come every year. We spend so much time and effort preparing for the big day, and then it is gone. Yes, celebrating Christ's arrival is well worth the wait, effort, and preparation. But once the day comes and goes, I often come down with a case of the after-Christmas blues. The anticipation is over, and the big event has passed. Now what?

Well, just as we waited with hopeful expectation for the arrival of Christmas, we now get to live out the real thing, waiting with hopeful expectation for the soon arrival of our coming King. Christmas was only a taste, a foreshadow of the good that is to come. The real celebration is coming soon, and I wait with bated breath for the day my Messiah comes for me. As we face the momentary struggles of this fallen world, let's remember that they are but the beginning of the incredible stories that we will tell of God's goodness when we get home to our true country.

Let the weary world rejoice! Christ has come, and He is coming back. Amen, Maranatha (which means "come, oh Lord!").

- Pastor Nate Morris

Pastor Nate Morris

lives in the mountains of Colorado with his wife Jen, and children Caleb, Zoe, and Josiah. Having grown up in the Colorado mountains, he has a special place in his heart for reaching and transforming mountain communities with the gospel. He is the lead pastor of Mountain Life Calvary Chapel, with locations in Vail and Glenwood Springs, Colorado. He hosts a podcast, "The Nate Morris Podcast," which can be found on all major podcast platforms. For more information on Pastor Nate, scan the QR below to connect with him online and on social media.

Facebook: nate.morris.9047
Instagram: @natemorris1
Podcast: anchor.fm/nate-morris1
Website: pastorn8.com

Mountain Life Publishing is a ministry of Mountain Life Calvary Chapel in Colorado. For more information on Mountain Life, our church, programs, internship possibilities and more, visit our website at https://mountainlife.church.

Please also check out Mountain Life Worship for original heart-felt songs of renewal and revival. Mountain Life Worship's original music is available on Apple Music, Spotify, and wherever you listen to music.

Made in the USA
Columbia, SC
01 December 2024

5f0ac8c7-84fe-48a2-a8f2-3284b4371333R01